GRIEVE NOT THE SPIRIT

A Treatise on Sin, Righteousness and Judgment

George (Jed) Smock

The Campus Ministry USA

Terre Haute IN

The Campus Ministry USA
PO BOX 3845
Terre Haute, IN 47803
Brojed@aol.com

Book Layout © 2014 BookDesignTemplates.com

Grieve Not The Spirit/Smock. – 3rd edition.

ISBN-13: 978-1541137363

Dedication

In memory of the late Mr. Harry Conn for girding up the loins of my mind.

TABLE OF CONTENTS

Introduction: The Broken Heart of God…….7

1. Convict of Sin………………………...15

2. Convince of Righteousness………...... 39

3. Convince of Judgment………………...……67

4. Conclusion: God's Perpetual Grief………...…97

Introduction:
The Broken Heart of God

God undoubtedly had great expectations for Adam, his image-bearer, when on the sixth day of creation he pronounced that everything he had made was very good. God and man had a time of delightful fellowship together in the Garden of Eden. Suddenly and unexpectedly, man betrayed his Creator and turned to God's arch-enemy Satan. Imagine God's utter disappointment and great sorrow when he had to drive man out of the garden for his own good, lest he eat of the tree of life and live forever in his fallen condition.

Since then, man, the crown of God's creation, has continued to bring unspeakable grief to God by thwarting his Maker's attempts to establish a loving relationship with him. Sixteen centuries after Adam's rebellion, the wickedness of man had become too great on the earth that "it repented the Lord that he had made man on the earth, and it grieved him at his heart" (Gen 6:6). So God had to destroy mankind in the flood and started over again with Noah. Sadly, Noah's generation also miserably failed God.

God called Abraham out of Ur of the Chaldees in order to develop the nation of Israel as his chosen people, from whom would come the Savior of mankind. But God was consistently grieved with the great majority of the nation and experienced great agitation of mind in having to bring about judgments against them, time and time again. Being longsuffering, he strove with man by sending prophets to warn the people and call them back to him; but they brutally killed his prophets. Finally, he sent his Son who was "a man of sorrows, and acquainted with grief" (Isa 53:3). Because of man's sin and unwillingness to lovingly fellowship with his Maker, Jesus wept and lamented over his people; but nevertheless they rejected him and delivered him up to be crucified. The sorrow and suffering of our Savior over man culminated when he bore man's sin on that cruel cross of Calvary.

The Father's Advocate

Jesus forewarned his disciples of his rejection, crucifixion, and departure from the world. In an effort to calm their fears, Jesus promised them 'another Comforter," who is the Holy Spirit. The Comforter was to lead them into all truth and enable them to bear witness of the truth to all men. The Holy Spirit and man were to be co-laborers in reconciling the world to God.

Jesus explained the Holy Spirit's threefold work in the world:

And when he is come, he will reprove (convict, convince) the world of sin, ...because they believe not on me; of righteousness, because I go to my Father, and ye see me no more; of judgment, because the prince of this world is judged (John 16:8-11).

The word translated Comforter in the King James Version is the Greek word, *Parakletos*, which may also be rendered *Advocate*. Jesus Christ is the sinner's advocate with the Father. The Holy Spirit is the Father's advocate to plead his case with mankind.

Charles Finney, America's great revivalist and theologian, defined *convince* or reprove as "a legal term meaning the summing up of an argument and establishing or demonstrating of the sinner's guilt. Thus, the strivings of the Spirit of God with man are not a physical scuffling, but a debate; a strife not of body with body, but of mind with mind, the action and reaction of vehement argumentation."

The Holy Spirit, according to Finney, exerts "moral power to pursue the sinner step by step with truth, to hunt him from his refuges of lies, to constrain him by the force of argument alone, to convince him to yield up his selfishness and dedicate himself to the service of God"

The Bible teaches that there are three different agents working in the conversion of the soul. The primary agent is the Spirit of God. Another agent is the minister or the one who is the messenger bringing the truth of the Word of God. The third agent is the sinner himself. The actual change is the sinner's personal act. "Ye have purified your souls in obeying the truth" (I Peter 1:22). The Holy Spirit influences and convinces the sinner to turn to God. "Of his own will begat he us with the word of truth" (James 1:18). A secondary agent is the minister or messenger who presents the truth. Paul said, "I have begotten you through the gospel" (I Cor. 4:15).

Man is a moral agent who has the capacity to resist any and every truth. Sin is moral evil that can only be conquered by men responding to the truth. Finney explains, "Whatever, therefore, hinders the truth from producing its sanctifying effect grieves the Holy Spirit, just in proportion to his desire to have it produce that effect."

The Church's Offense

The Apostle Paul warned the church that it should neither grieve nor quench the Holy Spirit (Eph. 4:30; I Thess. 5:19). To grieve him is to resist the light and energy which he brings to the mind of man. The Holy Spirit is a moral agent with sensibilities who experiences sorrow, distress and anguish over man's rebellion. To quench the Holy Spirit is to resist his mental impressions to the point of extinguishing his light and energy. It is to put out the fire which he longs to light in the souls of men. The ministry of the Holy Spirit has been a major emphasis in our generation. But in what has been labeled the full gospel movement, the stress has not been on the convicting ministry of the Holy Spirit, but rather on seeking the Holy Spirit's manifestations through speaking in tongues and the gifts of prophecy, healing, etc. Unfortunately these gifts have been too often abused. The Evangelicals, on the other extreme, have altogether denied that these gifts are for the modern church.

The Pentecostals, Charismatics, and Evangelicals, alike, have a common error – they have quenched the convicting ministry of the Holy Spirit. They have contrived new and better methods to win the world to Christ. These methods speak little on the subjects of sin, of righteousness and of judgement. Much is said of God's love and willingness to accept the sinner just as he is. This new way attracts large numbers to the churches. It also enables Christians to escape the persecution that Jesus promised would come to those who walked and witnessed in the Spirit: "These things have I spoken unto you, that ye should not be offended. They shall put you out of the synagogues: yea, the time cometh, that whosoever killeth you will think that he doeth God service" (John 16:1-2).

But the church has ignored the Lord's warning. It has been offended. When the offense came, the church changed its methods and message. The Holy Spirit has been seen as one who mollifies the world instead of convicting it. The Holy Spirit has become grieved because he is being replaced with another spirit, one who refuses to reprove sin, declare righteousness and warn of judgment. This false spirit has no relation to the One who empowered humble men to "turn the world upside down" and fearlessly face death with the gospel of Jesus Christ. This spirit is in error and instead of confronting the world, conforms to it. It is a spirit that bears no resemblance to the mighty Holy Spirit of God revealed and manifested in the glorious Book of Acts. It is a spirit that runs on high tech, mass media, expensive gimmicks and cheap thrills.

1

Convict of Sin

Jesus said the Holy Spirit would convict of sin "because they believe not on me." Noah Webster defined *convict*: "to convince of sin; to prove or determine to be guilty as by conscience."

Jesus confronted the scribes and Pharisees with their own sin when they brought to him the adulterous woman. "And they …being *convicted* by their own conscience, went out one by one" (John 8:9). When reproved of their sin, they hardened their hearts. We find this pattern throughout the New Testament that most people, when confronted with their guilt, are impenitent. The adulterous woman, on the other hand, chose not to justify her sin, but acknowledged the Lordship of Christ.

Jesus said, "The world cannot hate you; but me it hateth, because I testify of it, that the works thereof are evil" (John 7:7). So, if Jesus testified to the world that men's lives were evil, should not his disciples do the same? Paul affirms that God's purpose in sending his own Son was to "condemn sin in the flesh" (Rom 8:3).

What Sin?

If we are to labor effectively with the Holy Spirit, we must have a correct understanding of sin. Sin is defined as "transgression of the law" (I John 3:4). Sin, then, is a choice to deliberately and intentionally rebel against divine government. Sin is not a substance we inherit at birth, but it is a decision to live selfishly instead of lovingly toward others, as God intended for us to live.

Many misinterpret Jesus' statement, "....of sin, because they believe not on me." They believe that Jesus is teaching that men are primarily condemned because of rejecting Christ, not for breaking the moral law. Therefore, they "just preach Jesus" and encourage men to accept him immediately, instead of first dealing with their transgressions.

Actually, Jesus is teaching that because men reject him as Savior, their transgressions are not forgiven, and they are still subject to eternal death. Men are condemned to hell when they sin against the light of nature and their consciences. Rejection of Christ greatly intensifies men's guilt, but rejecting Christ is not the source of their guilt. If not believing in Jesus were the only sin that damned souls, then the heathen which have not heard the gospel would have to be excused by a just God. But Paul makes clear in the Roman letter that all men are without excuse.

Evangelicals are advised to offer Christ to people unconvinced of their sin (rebellion). What would we think of the doctor who haphazardly offered medication or surgery to people? The physician first must diagnose his patient's problem (sin); next he gives the prognosis (death); finally, he wants to give him some hope (the Great Physician). One should not speak of healing until the patient is first convinced that he is sick.

This analogy must not be taken too far. Sin is not a physical ailment, but an immoral choice. The sin problem cannot be cured by a "gospel pill", but by a choice to change the direction of one's life and to put one's faith in the person and work of Christ.

Reproving, Rebuking, and Exhorting

Even among those who acknowledge that it is the ministry of the Holy Spirit to convince men of sin, few appreciate the responsibility of the believer to work alongside the Spirit in accomplishing this goal. Since he is the Spirit of Truth, he will use the medium of the believer (who is supposed to be filled with the Spirit) to bring conviction to the conscience of the unbeliever. So the Christian needs to be sure he has the right message, backed up with the holy character that will reprove the world of sin.

We need to "preach the Word--reprove, rebuke, and exhort" (II Timothy 4:2). In today's message, as little as possible is said about sin. What used to be called sin is more likely to be labeled "hurts" or "problems." Certainly sinners may be hurting and have problems, but if they are going to be helped, they must acknowledge their sin to God and confess their faults one to another that they may be healed.

When the 120 were filled with the Holy Ghost in the upper room on the Day of Pentecost, devout Jews of every nation gathered together with the disciples to observe what was happening. They were utterly amazed because the disciples were speaking in the languages of their native countries. Some Jews mocked; others wanted to know what all this meant.

Peter stood up, but he did not testify, "Oh, I just had the most wonderful experience; I have received my prayer language." No, he began to preach–calling the crowd's attention to the prophets of old, signs of judgement and the resurrection and ascension of Jesus. Finally, he put his finger on the House of Israel. "Know assuredly that God hath made that same Jesus, whom ye have crucified, both Lord and Christ" (Acts 2:36). When they heard this, they were pricked in their hearts and convicted of their sin.

If Peter had not accused the Jews of murdering the Holy One, they would not have been convicted. Peter did not have the lights lowered and the music playing softly in order to produce a certain mood as he issued an invitation. Instead he plunged the sword of the Spirit's convincing truth into their hearts and made them cry out in agony, "What shall we do?" they asked. They gave their own altar call as they sought to be freed from sins, slavery and bondage. Peter then commanded them, "Repent and be baptized every one of you in the name of Jesus Christ for the remission of sins, and ye shall receive the gift of the Holy Ghost" (Acts 2:37-38).

In Acts, Chapter 3, after healing the lame man in the temple, Peter accused the men of Israel of murdering the Prince of Life and ordered them, "Repent and be converted, that your sins may be blotted out." The religious leaders arrested him, but meanwhile about 5,000 were converted.

War Against God

In Acts, Chapter 5, the apostles preached in the temple, and the chief priests had them arrested and brought before the council. Peter accused the priests of slaying Jesus, a Prince and a Savior "for to give repentance to Israel, and forgiveness of sin."

When the Jews heard, "…they were cut to the heart (convicted), and took counsel to slay the apostles." But Gamaliel, one of the leading councilmen, was able to give the apostles a little space. The priests were content to beat them and let them go, commanding them to speak no more in Jesus' name. But the apostles departed, "rejoicing that they were counted worthy to suffer for his name. And daily in the temple, and in every house, they ceased not to teach and preach Jesus Christ."

Despite the persecution, as Jesus had prophesied, the Holy Spirit was there to comfort the disciples. They were not offended even when put out of the synagogues and beaten. It is evident that the comforting presence of the Holy Spirit is to them who are persecuted for their aggressive faith, and for those who oppose sin.

Finally, the opposition to the Christians culminated in Stephen's arrest and defense before the council and high priest. He calmly related the history of Israel's unbelief and rebellion and consequent rejection by God. Suddenly, Steven accused his persecutors of being stiff-necked and uncircumcised in hearts and ears, of resisting the Holy Ghost, of persecuting and killing the prophets, of betraying and murdering Jesus and of breaking the law. When they heard this, the Jews were "cut to the heart." Evidently, they realized their guilt; but instead of repenting, they gnashed their teeth and stoned him to death.

And this is the condemnation, that light is come into the world, and men loved darkness rather than light, because their deeds were evil. For everyone that doeth evil hateth the light, neither cometh to the light, lest his deeds should be reproved (John 3:19-20).

Stephen's light was so bright that all who sat in the council saw that his face was glowing as the face of an angel. Yet they hated his life so much that they tried to snuff out his influence. They declared war on God!

Charles Finney called this type of reaction to truth, "the heinous sin of impenitence." Finney explained,

When the claims of God are revealed to the mind, it must necessarily yield to them, or strengthen itself in sin. It must, as it were, gird itself up, and struggle to resist the claims of duty. This strengthening of sin under light is the particular form of sin called impenitence.

Impenitence essentially consists of cleaving to self-indulgence under light.

Saul of Tarsus, who stood by as Stephen was martyred, continued to take the lead in the war against God by "making havoc of the church, entering into every house, and haling men and women committed them to prison" (Acts 8:3). But as he was on the road to Damascus to arrest more Christians, a light brighter than the sun appeared unto him, and the Lord accused Saul of persecuting him. Paul finally reacted positively to the truth and came to the light.

Attrition or Contrition?

Often ministers of the gospel are discouraged when they do not see mass conversions like those in the Book of Acts. They forget that history shows, and Jesus warned, that most men would resist rather than receive the convicting power of the Holy Spirit. Ministers must accept this, and they must come to an understanding of how the Holy Spirit works with the sinner.

The Holy Spirit provides the friction which rubs against the sinner's conscience. Initially, the sinner will often resist this rubbing, then the Holy Spirit steps up his activity and begins to grind away at the sinner's conscience, but still the sinner resists. The Spirit may lay siege to the sinner's conscience and carry on battle until there is a gradual wearing or weakening of the sinner's will, and, hopefully, his heart is broken and he surrenders to his Sovereign God.

Theologians use the term contrition to describe the sinner's surrender. Contrition is the repentance of sin perfected by the love of God, which makes a man shun and hate sin. It is a deep sorrowful experience for having displeased God by behaving sinfully. This godly sorrow results in a sincere hatred of sin and a resolve not to sin again.

Contrition is a necessary condition in order to be pardoned by God. Contrition is genuine repentance in contrast to *attrition*, which is false repentance motivated by fear of punishment or rejection by God, or by the pro-spect of personal gain or advantage to becoming a Christian. The merely attrite sinner has been worn down, but not pulver-ized. He resists so hard that he forms calluses upon his conscience, until the Holy Spirit is grieved away because he cannot break the sinner without violating his will, which is something the Holy Spirit will nev-er do in the matter of man's salvation.

King Saul and Judas felt attrition over their sins, but instead of becoming contrite, they both committed suicide. Peter and King Da-vid, on the other hand, experienced contrition over their sins. David affirmed in Psalms 51:17, "The sacrifices of God are a broken spirit: A broken and a contrite heart, O God, thou wilt not despise."

Unconditional Surrender

In the early days of my ministry, I was quick to push people into "professions of faith" or praying the "sinner's prayer," but as I stud-ied the Bible more, it became obvious that many of my "converts" had never reached contrition over their sins. In fact, some had never experienced attrition. Convinced that true converts were more important to God than evangelistic numbers, I strove to be more sensitive to the workings of the Holy Spirit in the life of the sinner.

Paul was a freshman in business aviation at Ohio State University. When I met him in 1987, my evangelistic efforts had been in conformity with those of the Holy Spirit for a number of years, yet watching Paul's experience was to give me a deeper understanding and appreciation of the Holy Spirit's role in conversion. Paul had read a few gospel tracks, and he regularly watched a television preacher. When he heard Brother Max Lynch preaching on the campus lawn in spring, 1986, Paul was wavering between atheism and theism. Paul was amazed that an educated man in his late fifties would spend his time preaching to a crowd of jeering college students.

"I was impressed that he was not out golfing," Paul said. "I remembered the scriptures that Brother Max quoted: 'Be ye holy for I am Holy,' and, 'Except ye repent you will all likewise perish.'"

Later, Paul heard me preaching from my favorite text for college students, I Corinthians

6:9-10: "Be not deceived: neither fornicators, nor idolaters, nor adulterers, nor effeminate, nor abusers of themselves with mankind, nor thieves, nor covetous, nor drunkards, nor revilers, nor extortioners, shall inherit the kingdom of God."

Paul recalled "I knew that if what Brother Jed was saying was true, I was in trouble. I also intuitively knew that some things I did were wrong. I began to see the vanity of sin and cut down on sinning."

Paul concluded that atheism was not a reasonable option.

Driving in his pickup truck in February, 1987, Paul professed faith in Christ and claimed the salvation experience.

One day, while I was ministering at Ohio State, Paul and I discussed sin, holiness, and temptation. Paul asked me, "What if you keep on doing the sin?"

I quoted the promise given to us in I Corinthians 10:13: "There hath no temptation taken you but such as is common to man: But God is faithful, who will not suffer you to be tempted above that ye are able; but will with the temptation also make a way to escape, that ye may be able to bear it."

"Paul," I explained, "if you are tempted to cheat, be honest. If you are tempted to lie, tell the truth. If you are tempted to lust, think about something else. Just say 'no' to sin."

Most Christians probably would have quoted I John 2:1 to Paul: "if any man sin, we have an advocate with the Father, Jesus Christ the righteous." I would not dispute that forgiveness is a great blessing, but people need to hear that Jesus also promised *deliverance* from sin.

Paul began coming to our Bible studies and church services in fall, 1987. I accepted that he had become a Christian in February. Paul was a serious Bible reader and truth seeker. By everything I could see, Paul demonstrated the fruit of the Spirit. He was faithful, reliable, and responsible. I hoped for a church full of men just like him.

Little did I know that Paul was only in a Romans Chapter 7 experience and had not yet been converted. However, the Holy

Spirit knew, and he continued to work on Paul's heart.

In the Bible studies and sermons over the next few months, I emphasized Biblical holiness and concentrated on themes of sin, righteousness and judgment.

The Holy Spirit was faithful to complete the work that he had begun, and within a year, Paul submitted to the point of contrition. Today, Paul's testimony is one of total victory over sin.

Paul developed into a powerful lay preacher. He graduated from Ohio State in the winter of 1991. He spent the following spring boldly preaching in the same spot where, five years earlier, the Holy Spirit had begun to convict him of sin, righteousness and judgment.

Paul's testimony gave me more confidence that if I was faithful to preach the truth, the Holy Spirit could and would do a complete work in the soul of those who hear me.

Spurious Conversions

The minister of the Gospel must be determined to preach with conviction regardless of his listeners' reactions. Too often Christians, in attempting to present the gospel, weaken the message to the point of no longer declaring the truth. Therefore, the Holy Spirit is frustrated in his efforts to convince of sin, and impenitent souls continue in their mad rush for hell. A softer message may increase church membership, but it will decrease the number of true conversions. Woe unto the minister who treads such dangerous ground. He will be reproved of God on Judgement Day for fighting against the Holy Spirit.

Men-pleasers are opposed to any preaching that results in condemnation--both to those who do not profess the faith and to those who do. They are fond of quoting John 3:17: "For God sent not his Son into the world to condemn the world; but that the world through him might be saved"--thus the saying, "Jesus saves, he doesn't condemn."

They ignore John 3:18: "He that believeth not is condemned already, because he hath not believed in the name of the only begotten Son of God." The true message must warn men that they are judged guilty and in danger of eternal jeopardy. One only offers a pardon to those who are already condemned, not to those who insist they have never done anything deserving hell.

An evangelical offering pardon to a sinner unconvinced of his guilt is much like President Ford pardoning Richard Nixon, concerning the Watergate Affair. Nixon had never been declared guilty by any court of law, or even formally charge of a crime by a court, nor did Nixon ever admit to guilt of any criminal offense. He admitted to mistakes and errors of judgement, and even showed some remorse for certain actions. But it was irresponsible of President Ford, to entrust with the execution of laws, to pardon a man who was merely generally assumed to be guilty. Ultimately, such action only generates a lack of respect for due process of law.

There is a gross disregard for due process in the evangelical community today. We have preachers, who are supposed to be responsible for upholding God's law, offering pardons to people without insisting on admission of guilt or demanding evidence of true repentance. God's court has already accused the sinner and condemned him to death; but until the sinner acknowledges his guilt and condemnation, ministers are not acting justly or wisely to offer him a pardon, because before God exempts the individual from the death penalty for sin, he demands an admission of guilt and a willingness to change.

Since the Holy Spirit is often quenched, multitudes have come into the church without being convicted of their sin and coming to true repentance and faith. Prematurely, men have been lead in a sinner's prayer and pronounced "saved."

In a typical evangelistic crusade of our day, it would not be unusual to hear a conversation around the altar something like the following:

Sinner: "I asked Jesus into my heart, but I don't feel like I am saved."

Evangelist: "What you feel is not important, what counts is what the Bible says. John 1:12 reads, 'For as many as receive him, to them gave he the power to become the sons of God, even to them that believe his name.'"

Sinner: "I still don't think that I am a child of God."

Evangelist: "Are you calling God a liar? John 3:16 says, 'For God so loved the world, that he gave his only begotten son, that whosoever believeth in him should not perish, but have everlasting life.' The Bible says it; if you believe it, then that settles it. You are saved. I just prayed with you."

It is arrogant for anyone to try to convince others they are saved. This is intruding on the office of the Holy Spirit. The Bible teaches, "The Spirit itself beareth witness with our spirit, that we are the children of God" (Rom.8:16). Yet many evangelists seem to think it is their calling to travel the country assuring impenitent sinners and carnal professors that their sins are forgiven based on answering an altar call and repeating a prayer. The same evangelist would condemn a Roman Catholic priest for acting as a mediator between God and man, when they do the same thing merely under different authorities, structures and rituals.

Evangelists would better serve the church if they would challenge people to question their salvation in light of the conditions of justification, instead of attempting to give them assurance of salvation.

In Acts, chapter 8, Philip the Evangelist had a great revival in Samaria, including miracles, which affected the whole city; and a large number believed and were baptized. Peter and John came down from Jerusalem to lay hands on the believers for them to receive the Holy Ghost. When Simon saw that the Holy Ghost was given by the laying on of hands, he offered them money, saying, "Give me also this power, that on whomsoever I lay hands, he may receive the Holy Ghost."

But Peter said unto him, "Thy money perish with thee.... Thou hast neither part nor lot in this matter: for thy heart is not right in the sight of God. Repent and pray to the Lord that if possible, this may be forgiven you. For I see that you are in the gall of bitterness and the bond of iniquity."

Simon is like so many who have been swept into the church through the Pentecostal revival and the Charismatic renewal movement. It seems obvious that Simon was primarily seeking the power, the gifts and the supernatural, rather than a righteous relationship with the Lord.

Jesus had to deal with the multitude that followed him for the loaves and fishes--for what they could get from him, instead of what they could give. When his preaching brought conviction of sin and called for righteous living, the crowds had a way of dwindling. They wanted everything but the truth, which demanded a life of self-denial.

He That Hath an Ear, Let Him Hear

The apostles effectively used the miracles in the Book of Acts to gain attention to their message, minister to the needs of people and witness to the power of the resurrected Christ and the Holy Spirit in their lives. But their main concern was to proclaim a message that would transform lives; this is what is so often lacking in our generation. The gifts of the Spirit have been used to expose sickness and disease, but not sin. Ministers who have proudly proclaimed the presence of the Holy Spirit in their service, have themselves, time and time again, been exposed as hypocrites. Churches have been founded primarily to give people an opportunity to express the gifts of the Spirit such as prophecy or healing, but rarely has this gift been used to bring forth a message that will convict and judge the sinner.

Paul admonished the Corinthians that when the whole church comes together, "If all prophecy, and there come in one that believeth not, or one unlearned, he is *convinced* of all, he is *judge*d of all: And thus are the secrets of his heart made manifest; and so falling down on his face he will worship God, and report that God is in you of a truth," (I Cor.14:24-25).

Typically, in churches where prophecy is given free rein, we hear only words of approval and acceptance. Of course, Paul did teach that "he that prophesieth speaketh unto men to edification, and exhortation and comfort" (I Cor.14:3). However, this should not eliminate rebuke, a strong, or even a harsh word. These words are also edifying and comforting, when received and acted upon.

Those lacking in understanding often claim that the Holy Spirit never condemns believers, he merely convicts. Their proof text is Romans 8:1: "There is therefore now no condemnation to them which are in Christ Jesus" but they fail to quote the rest of the verse; "who walk not after the flesh, but after the Spirit." Granted, some modern translations omit the last part of Romans 8:1, but verse four of chapter eight also includes the qualifications. So, professing believers who are governed by their fleshly appetites are condemned. Actually, they stand in greater condemnation than those who have never seen the truth, because guilt is always measured according to knowledge. The greater the knowledge, the greater the guilt. (Luke 12:47-48)

Many scholars consider the seven churches of the Book of Revelation to be typical of the modern church. Hear what the Spirit was saying to the seven churches. Although the Holy Spirit does have some positive things to say about each, except the Laodiceans, five of the seven churches are reproved for sin and called to repentance under the threat of dire judgments. The Church of Smyrna is warned of great impending tests, trials and tribulations. The Church of Philadelphia is commended for having "kept the Word of my patience," but is warned to "hold fast which thou hast." The Spirit makes clear that all the churches need to live righteously. Nothing is said to any of them about the Spirit's pleasure or presence in their worship services.

Are we really hearing what the Spirit is saying to the churches, or are the churches quenching the Spirit's desire to convince of sin, righteousness and judgment? Is God really as pleased with the church as we are hearing or are we only hearing what pleases us?

2

Convinced of Righteousness

Jesus Christ was a preacher of righteousness. When he prepared to depart from the
world, he promised to send the Holy Spirit
to convince the world of righteousness, because he was going back to the Father and
they would see him no more.

The ultimate intention of the Holy Spirit, as
revealed in the Scriptures, is to sanctify the
souls of men. Men are to be saved by "the
sanctification of the Spirits through belief in
the truth" (II Thessalonians 2:13). Sanctification, righteousness and holiness are terms
which mean basically the same thing: the
enablement by God's Spirit to voluntarily
and lovingly obey God. Jesus said, "When
he, the Spirit of Truth, is come, he will guide
you into all truth" (John 16:13). Truth is the
influence the Holy Spirit uses to sanctify the
souls of men.

God has always had a standard to which he
holds himself and all moral beings; this
standard is righteousness. Noah Webster
defined righteousness as "purity of heart and

rectitude of life; conformity of heart and life to the Divine law. It includes all that we call justice, honesty and virtue, with holy affections; in short, it is true religion." God himself is righteous. This is the root of man's moral obligation to him. Should God ever cease to be righteous, he would no longer be deserving of our service. The true believer does not just worship God because he is almighty, but because of his perfect rectitude and faithfulness. God is deserving of our devotion, because he always uses his power morally and lovingly.

From the beginning, Satan has influenced man to question the righteousness of God. Satan deceived Eve into believing that God was withholding something good, which would make her life happier. Jesus was accused by his contemporaries of being an imposter, possessed by the devil, a seducer and lawbreaker.

Jeremiah acutely expresses the pathos of God in imploring Israel during her death agony as a nation. "What iniquity have your fathers found in me, that they are gone far from me, and have walked after vanity, and are become vain?" (Jer.2:5).

Indeed, we have a remarkable picture here of the great God, the Creator, Ruler and Sustainer of the Universe, humbling himself before rebellious men, challenging them to plead their case against him. God was asking if they had ever found anything cruel, oppressive or unjust in his laws or anything unkind or tyrannical in his government.

God wondered that they had become gross idolaters and adulterers. Even the priests sought not the Lord; the pastors broke his law; and the prophets prophesied by Baal, and walked after unprofitable things. Still God promised to continue to plead with their children's children.

The behavior of the people had become so wicked that even the heavens were astonished, shocked, appalled, and horrified over Israel's iniquity. God could not understand what had happened to Israel, "I had planted thee a noble vine, wholly a right seed: how then art thou turned unto the degenerate plant of a strange vine unto me?" (Jer.2:21)

The Lord had such high expectations for Israel, but she had become such a bitter disappointment to God. Whatever means God had tried to bring her back proved in vain: "In vain have I smitten your children; they received no correction: your own sword hath devoured your prophets, like a destroying lion" (Jer.2:30)

Despite her rebellion and God's striving, Israel still had the audacity to maintain her innocence. "I have not sinned," she claimed. (Jer.2:35)

Like Israel of old, sinners of our day protest that they are good people and foolishly charge God with being unjust in his dealing with men. Even more pathetically, carnal professing Christians with irrational doctrines concerning sin and righteousness malign and misrepresent the character of the Father and his Son, who suffered so much in the hands of wicked men. Thereby, they grieve the Spirit of Truth by representing God as arbitrary, vindictive and inscrutable instead of reasonable, magnanimous and personal.

The Atonement

The Holy Spirit was given to testify to the righteousness of God. And we, also, are to bear witness of his righteousness. The atonement of Christ was made "to declare…God's righteousness: that he might be just, and be the justifier of him which believeth in Jesus." The atonement offered God the opportunity for the highest manifestation of virtue by sacrificing his own Son. God substituted the suffering of Christ on the cross for the eternal punishment of sinner. Had God damned all men as they deserve, he would have been perceived as merely severe and unmerciful. Had he forgiven men only on the basis of their repentance, then his justice and veracity would have been called into question, because he had repeatedly warned from the beginning that the wages of sin is death. The atonement gave God the occasion to righteously demonstrate both his mercy and his justice, thus exhibiting a loving nature unparalleled in the universe. To any serious thinker, the cross proves God's holy love and convicts him of his own selfishness in committing the transgressions which made the atonement necessary. But few are careful to make this point when witnessing to the sinner. Instead, the over-eager proselytizer says, "Jesus died for all your sins--past, present and future. Now all you have to do is accept it." The cross is presented as a cheap and easy fire escape instead of that great act of benevolence, which was intended to break the power of sin and subdue the heart of the unrighteous.

The Holy Spirit manifests Jesus Christ, "whom God hath set forth to be a propitiation through faith in his blood, to declare his righteousness for the remission of sins that are *past.* To declare, I say, at this time his righteousness: that he might be just, and the justifier of him which believeth in Jesus" (Romans 3:25-26).

No rational being could be convinced that God is righteous if a believer is automatically forgiven for future sins. What would we think of a judge who said the following to a confessed thief? "Because you have admitted to your crimes, I pardon you, not only for your past thefts, but for any crimes you commit in the future-and surely you will steal again for no man can be completely honest. But you have acknowledged me as your judge; therefore, I am going to release you." Such a pardon would be a mockery of both justice and mercy. Yet, this is the attitude many Christians have concerning the character of the Righteous Judge of the Universe. They believe that they can commit sin with virtual impunity, losing, perhaps, their fellowship with God, but never their relationship of right standing with him.

Law is Not a Dirty Word

The moral law is the permanent definition of sin and righteousness (Romans 3:20, 7:7; I John 3:4: James 2:8-9). It requires that we love God supremely, and our neighbor equally. The Apostle James called it the royal law. The Ten Commandments show what love demands. For example, if a man loves God, he will not use his name in vain: if he loves his neighbor as himself, he will not steal from him. All beings in the universe, including God, are supposed to be governed by the law of love. This moral law promotes the highest well-being of all and works to prevent the highest misery of all.

Had man been willing to live according to the law of God, it would have been well with him and his children for all generations. And it would have made God exceedingly happy. But man in his selfishness has consistently rebelled against God's authority and bountiful love. God sent his prophets to call man to repentance, but man killed the prophets. Finally, God sent his Son, but man rejected and killed his Savior.

Antinomians teach that since the New Testament came into effect a believer is no longer obligated to keep the moral law. If this is so, then Christ suffered in vain. Isaiah prophesied of the coming of the Messiah: "The Lord is well pleased for his righteousness' sake: he will magnify the law, and make it honorable" (Isa.42:21). Christ did not come to remove the believer's obligation to obey the moral law. Instead his sacrificial death provided the loving motive to enable the Christian to obey. If God intended to remove man's moral responsibility to the law, he could simply have arbitrarily repealed its precepts and sanctions without any conditions including an atonement. But in that case justice would have lost, and lawlessness would have won. Christ's atonement was resorted to as a way of reconciling forgiveness with justice. Forgive man without an atonement, mercy may be magnified, but justice suffers. Execute the full penalty of the law against all sinners, justice is magnified, but mercy suffers. Substitute the suffering of Christ for the punishment of sinners and both mercy and justice are exalted. Then the dignity of the law is upheld and man can be reconciled to God on the conditions of repentance and faith in Christ's atoning work. Oh, what a marvelous plan of redemption. Let antinomian enemies of the cross be accursed!

Man has never been, nor will he ever be, without obligation to the moral law, before the cross or after, on earth or in heaven. Charles Finney explained, "God has no right to give up the moral law. He cannot discharge us from the duty of love to God and love to man for this is right in itself. And unless God will alter the whole moral constitution of the universe, so as to make that right which is wrong, he cannot give up the claims of the moral law."

Teaching that God's moral law is impossible to keep is another contemporary heresy which thwarts the Holy Spirit's attempts to convince man that God is righteous. How could a righteous God give a law to man that he knew man could not keep and threaten him with eternal damnation for disobedience? Such a God would not be just, but a tyrant and a despot.

The Scriptures make clear that God fully expected man to obey him. With a heart-rending plea God laments, "O that there were such an heart in them, that they would fear me, and keep my commandments always, that it might be well with them, and with their children forever!" (Deut. 5:29).

God was not at all arbitrary in giving his law; he fully respected man's freedom. He only expected man to exercise his freedom responsibly for his own good and the good of his children.

Not only did God expect the people to keep the law but the people had promised to be obedient. When Moses told the people the words of the law, all the people answered with one voice, "All the words which the Lord hath said will we do" (Exodus 24:3).

Not only does the Holy Spirit convince man of God's righteousness, but he convinces man that he must be righteous; the Holy Spirit desires that man be right with God. What is salvation but a right relationship with God and one's fellows? Man's predicament is that his sin has separated him from his Maker and alienated him from his neighbor. But "God was in Christ, reconciling the world unto himself, not imputing their trespasses unto them... For he hath made him to be sin for us, who knew no sin; that we might be made the *righteousness* of God in him" (II Corinthians 5:19, 21). Jesus bore the consequences of our sins through his suffering and death, not only that he might justly and righteously offer us forgiveness, but also that we might be transformed into the character of Christ--made righteous.

Christ's atonement accomplished what the animal sacrifices of the Old Covenant failed to do. It provided the moral *influence* to make the believer habitually righteous. Under the old system, the Jew was to offer the best animal of his flock as a sacrifice for sin. The prize bull that had won the blue ribbons at the fair was to be brought and slain and the blood sprinkled on the altar.

What was the rationale of a blood sacrifice? Was God some bloodthirsty tyrant who refused to forgive sin without a blood offering to appease his wrath? No. The blood offering was to be an object lesson to the offender. When he saw this innocent animal suffering the consequences of his sin, an animal that he had nurtured and cared for, it was to make such an impression on his mind that he was to leave this worship service determined to sin no more. Since the life was in the blood, men found spilled blood a revolting sight. The idea was that men should be just as disturbed by the very thought of sin. But, the sacrifice was still merely a dumb animal; it could be replaced. So then the tendency was to forget the experience, and the individual soon returned to his selfish ways. The sacrificial system of old was very limited in what it could accomplish.

On our streets and highways, animals are often run over by cars. Typically people just drive on. Some might be a little bothered for a while, especially if someone's pet has been hit. But the incident will soon be forgotten because, after all, it is merely a brute.

A number of years ago I was driving home from a revival service. A college student, who had given his testimony during the service, was driving a car in front of me. Suddenly, he hit his brakes, but it was too late. He had hit a pedestrian. Naturally, I did not just drive on, because this was not an animal lying bleeding in the road, but a human being. Unfortunately, the man was dead. When the ambulance came to take the body, I realized I knew the man. It was my barber. Suddenly, the result of the careless driving and the jaywalking had a much greater impact on me. Because I have seen shed blood, the actual consequences of carelessness, I have been a more careful driver and pedestrian. After several years that incident is still branded in my memory. Hopefully, it had an even greater impression on the young driver.

Men need to comprehend how terribly sin has hurt God. This pain had been building in the soul of God since Adam. Men must see how the innocent Lamb of God became so burdened on the cross with all the sins of mankind he could take it no more; he cried out with a loud voice "It is finished," and he gave up the ghost. Our Savior's grief over sin culminated in his death from a broken, devastated heart.

When men see the appalling agony of the cross, it should have such an impact on their character, that their hearts will also be broken. They will be determined to sin no more. The terrible consequences about the death of Jesus Christ, great love for their Savior, and such a holy hatred of sin, that they will live a righteous life.

Sophists argue that God accounts us as righteous when we acknowledge faith in Christ, even though we will continue to sin until the time of death. Such men have never actually been to Calvary, or they could never hold such sin-excusing views. If it is, indeed, impossible for man to be habitually righteous, then the sinner has an excuse to sin. As a result, the Holy Spirit's ministry is diminished to encourage a man to maintain a tolerable level of disobedience.

The Bible was given to us to instruct us in righteousness (II Timothy 3:16). It is absurd to think, as so many do, that our manual for life would teach us that it is impossible for those who believe the book to live habitually righteous lives.

St. John wrote his epistle specifically to teach men not to sin (I John 2:1) John instructed, "If ye know that Jesus is righteous, ye know that everyone that doeth righteousness is born of him" (I John 2:29). Who does he believe is born again? They that act righteously. John makes perfectly clear that obedience is what separates a Christian from an unbeliever: "In this the children of God are manifest, and the children of the devil: whosoever doeth not righteousness is not of God" (I John 3:10). John is emphatic: "little children, let no man deceive you: he that doeth righteousness is righteous, even as he (Christ) is righteous" (I John 3:7). Notice John is addressing the little children, which would be the immature in faith, telling them that only those who practice righteousness have the righteousness of Christ. John concludes, "We know that whosoever is born of God sinneth not; but he that is begotten of God keepeth himself, and that wicked one toucheth him not" (I John 5:18).

The Sophist, to excuse his continuance in sin, desperately appeals to I John 1:8 "If we say that we have no sin, we deceive ourselves, and the truth is not in us." But this verse applies to an individual claiming to have no sin for which god will hold him accountable, while he continues to sin. The "we" speaking in this verse refers to the liars of verse six, those who claim to be Christians, but "walk in darkness" (practice sin), and obey not the truth. It is also possible that John is rebuking those who claim to have never sinned and therefore have no need of a Savior. If, in chapter one, verse eight, John is teaching that Christians never completely overcome sin in this lifetime, then he is contradicting the immediate context, which teaches that Jesus' blood cleanses from all unrighteousness, not to mention many other verses in his letter, a few of which already have been cited. It is preposterous to think that an inspired writer would state his purpose: "My little children, these things I write unto you, that ye sin not," but prelude this as impossible.

Only professing Christians could be convinced of such nonsense; the world has more sense. That is why, when a believer is exposed as a sinner, he is universally condemned by the world, but too often excused by the church.

Jews Versus Gentiles

Modern interpreters, unfamiliar with the historical setting in which Paul wrote his letters, miss one of the greatest themes of the New Testament, which is the conflict between the Jews and the Gentiles. The conflict was not simply with the Jews who denied that Jesus was the Christ. It also included the Jews who believed in Jesus as the Messiah, but who could not give up their commitment to the ceremonial law. The moral law shows us how to live. The ceremonial law, through animal sacrifices, symbolically provided the Jew the way of being restored to God's favor after breaking the moral law. But in the New Testament some Jewish believers in Jesus depended on their rituals and traditions more than the Messiah, who now had come to set them free from that yoke of bondage.

New Testament writers, who seem at times to make disparaging remarks on moral uprightness, moral law, and good works, are in truth not attacking these, but are attempting to show the futility of finding salvation through the rites and rituals of Judaism. This theme comes forth most strongly in the Galatian letter. The Judaizers were pressing for circumcision of all believers as a requirement of justification. Paul refutes them with many arguments, including the fact that Abraham was justified by faith, 430 years before the giving of the law: "Even as Abraham believed God, and it was accounted to him for righteousness" (Gal. 3:6).

Among the Roman church, there were legalists who taught that Christians must keep dietary laws and observe certain days, thus causing much controversy in the church. Paul reproves them by explaining that "the kingdom of God is not meat and drink; but *righteousness*, and peace, and joy in the Holy Ghost" (Romans 14:17). It is notable that Paul considers right action as part of a trinity of life in the Spirit. Unrighteousness will convict a man's conscience, thus robbing him of his peace of mind, without which there is no true joy. Jesus explained that we must keep his commandments for his joy to remain in us, and for our joy to be full (John 15:10-12).

The Holy Spirit reproves all attempts by man to be righteous without the grace of God. "Therefore by the deeds of the law there shall no flesh be justified in his sight: for by the law is the knowledge of sin" (Romans 3:20). Once having transgressed the law, man cannot simply decide to obey it and hope to be forgiven, because there is still the problem of his past sins, which can only be forgiven on the condition of repentance and faith in the atonement of Jesus Christ.

Antinomians like to appeal to Romans 6:14 out of context: "…for ye are not under the law, but under grace." But the first part of this verse is rarely quoted by the lawless: "For sin shall not have dominion over you." What if sin still does have dominion over a person? What is he under, law or grace? Law! The individual sinning daily in thought, word and/or deed is under law. He is trying to obey out of the principle of fear of punishment or hope of reward, which is always doomed to failure. He that is truly converted is free from the power of sin. He has the strength to habitually obey because he is operating under the greater principle of faith and love for God.

Romans chapter 7, reveals Paul's vain attempts to live righteously by the law-convicted of his sins, but not yet converted to Jesus Christ. Paul, as a Pharisee, was blameless concerning the outward keeping of the law. The Holy Spirit, in his strivings with Paul, finally revealed to him the implications of the 10th commandment and exposed the basic selfishness to which he was enslaved. Paul had come to understand the spirituality of the law which required him to love God supremely and his neighbor equally. He was struggling in his own efforts to conform to the demands of the law, but constantly failing. Finally, acknowledging his depravity, he cried, "O wretched man that I am! Who shall deliver me from the body of this death?" Certainly, not the law, for there is no power in it to either change the heart or forgive sin. It can only condemn. But then Paul apprehends the gospel which reveals the answer to his desperate question: "I thank God through Jesus Christ our Lord" (Rom.7:25).

In Romans chapter 8, Paul concludes that the righteousness of the law is fulfilled in him and all who believe in Jesus. The love of Christ and his sufferings on the cross had achieved what the law could not do, by breaking his heart (will). The atonement gave Paul the incentive and loving motive to change his purpose from serving self supremely to seeking first the highest good of God and his fellow man. Thus as a new creature in Christ, Paul began to live a life free from the power and dominion of sin.

The modern gospel is man-centered instead of God-centered. Evangelicals encourage unbelievers to become Christians that they might experience real happiness and have peace of mind. Although Jesus did come that we might have a more abundant life, our primary motive for following Christ should not be our personal happiness. The truly convinced person ultimately serves God because it is the right thing to do. It is only right that we should love him with all of our heart, soul, mind and strength, who has his given his life for us.

Put Out of the Synagogue

In the summer of 1985, I scheduled a number of weekend meetings in Memphis, Tennessee; Saturday morning I spoke in a businessmen's meeting, and Sunday morning I addressed the congregation of a large full gospel church. In both services, my messages on holiness and evangelism were well-received.

Sunday night, I was slated to speak in a smaller full gospel church. Upon arrival with my evangelistic team, we found the congregation, mostly women, milling around greeting and hugging one another. There were a lot of prolonged embraces with chattering, laughing and sobbing. Unable to locate the pastor, I politely asked one lady what time the service started.

"It has already started. We just arrive and start loving on one another," she giggled. She quickly told her friend that I was the guest speaker.

The friend squealed, "Oh, I just love to hug the preachers!" as she flung her huge body against mine.

I escaped and, to my relief, finally found the pastor. We spent about ten minutes discussing my ministry. He seemed enthusiastic and especially interested in my South Africa book.

Service began with what turned out to be a very long time of praise and worship. People continued to walk around, and women clustered in groups talking and praying with one another.

The pastor then began to operate in what many today would call the word of knowledge. He called out a number of illnesses and said those mentioned were to come forth and be healed.

One older lady went to the alar and the pastor determined that she had a "spirit of rejection." So a number of brethren gathered around her and began casting out a "spirit of suicide."

After that, the lady informed those praying for her that she was deaf. The pastor prayed, laying hands on her ears, and then he asked her if she could hear anything.

She responded, "No, I can't hear a thing."

They all prayed again, until she danced a jig back to her seat.

After a long hour and a half, I was called to the pulpit. I asked the people to open their Bibles to I John. I began to preach an expository sermon titled, *What is a Christian?* I preached this same sermon in churches many times before and since; it consisted of reading and expounding in many of the highlights of I John. The main point being that a Christian is one who obeys God, and anyone who does not obey, yet professes Christ, is a hypocrite. The message was mainly a theological argument for holiness of the heart. Nothing was said about the externals, and no personal rebukes were made on the church.

Near what was to be the close of the message, I read I John 3:19-21:

And hereby we know that we are of the truth and shall assure our hearts before him; for if our heart condemn us, God is greater than our heart and knoweth all things. Beloved, if our heart condemn us not then we have confidence toward God.

I explained, "If you feel convicted by this message, please don't walk away saying, 'That preacher condemned me.' For if our heart condemns us, how much more does God, who knows all? Friend, if you feel condemned by this message, you might just consider, it may be because you are condemned."

At this point, the pastor stood up and told me to stop preaching. Then he proceeded to apologize to his church for having me preach. As I walked down the aisle, I warned the pastor that he had rejected the truth. He told me to pack up my things and leave. The congregation began to applaud the pastor's action.

By this time, a member of our party could be contained no longer and stood up and rebuked the pastor. "You need to repent, you wimp." The whole church gasped in unbelief. With each new statement made, they all gasped again.

"Why have you people rejected the holiness message? Are you saying there's no sin among you?" (Gasp) "How many of you are fornicators?" (Gasp) "How many adulterers?" (Gasp) "Who is looking at pornography?" (Gasp) "You ministers of music up there with earrings on, you're not acting like men of God." (Gasp) "And all you women wandering around thinking you are prophetesses need to repent."

Then a number of men headed towards us, praying loudly in tongues. I intercepted them. I demanded that they speak to me in

English and correct my doctrine if they could. Finally, our things were packed, and as we left another one our team members shouted, "Ichabod!"

Jesus rightly said, "These things have I spoken unto you that ye should not be offended ....They shall put you out of the synagogues..." Paul added, "For God hath not called us to uncleanness, but onto holiness. He therefore that despiseth, despiseth not man, but God, who hath also given unto us his Holy Spirit" (I Thess. 4:7-8).

God's Great Blessing

Those who profess faith in Christ need to get their lives straight and stop making excuses for sin. They have to quit opposing the Holy Spirit's attempts to promote righteousness.

Paul exhorted the charismatic church at Corinth to, "Awake to righteousness and sin not; for some have not the knowledge of God: I speak this to your shame" (I Cor. 15:34).

It is a dishonor to the Holy Spirit that many so-called Spirit-filled churches have people with their hands raised, who are still dead in their trespasses and sin; people who boast of their power and authority over demons, sickness, disease and poverty, but are impotent when it comes to overcoming sin. "The righteous are bold as a lion" (Proverbs 28:1). The believers' real strength is in holiness and rectitude of character.

Jesus exhorted men to seek first the kingdom of God and his righteousness; and promised that then all things would be added unto them. But men are seeking first the material and physical blessings of this life. Few are interested in the greatest blessing God has to offer: "Unto you first God, having raised up his son Jesus, sent him to bless you, in turning away every one of you from his iniquities" (Acts 3:26). Like Simon the sorcerer, men are seeking the power of the Spirit to cast out demons, heal the sick, etc., but shun the moral power of righteous living. A truly spiritual man is a morally upright man.

Ultimately, what is the evidence of being filled with the Holy Spirit, but a holy life? Where the Holy Spirit dwells, there is not room for sin. There are many that seem to think that the Spirit-filled life consists primarily of saying the right words or speaking in tongues, casting out devils, prophesying and doing miracles. But Jesus reminded us that,

Not everyone that saith unto me, 'Lord, Lord,' shall enter into the kingdom of heaven; but he that doeth the will of my father which is in heaven. Many will say to me in that day, 'Lord, Lord, have we not prophesied in thy name? and in thy name have cast out devils? and in thy name done many wonderful works?' and then will I profess unto them, 'I never knew you: depart from me, ye that work iniquity' (Matt.7:21-23).

A true movement of the Holy Spirit will sweep away all sin, and sanctify men wholly, and prepare men to suffer affliction and reproach.

Thus saith the Lord: 'Let not the wise man glory in his wisdom, neither let the mighty man glory in his might. Let not the rich man glory in his riches; but let him that glorieth glory in this, that he understandeth and knoweth me, that I am the Lord which exercises lovingkindness, judgement, and righteousness in the earth: for in these things I delight,' saith the Lord (Jer.9:23-24).

3

CONVINCE OF JUDGMENT

The Holy Spirit will convince the world "of judgement because the prince of this world is judged" (John 16:11). Men who believe in Christ will escape the judgement of God, but those who believe not will certainly be doomed with the devil to the Lake of Fire.

The minister must work with the Holy Spirit to make it clear to the sinner that, without repentance and faith in Christ, his only future is eternal damnation.

No one in the Bible gave more warning on hell than Jesus: "And I say unto you my friends, be not afraid of them that kill the body, and after that have no more that they can do. But I will forewarn you whom ye shall fear: fear him, which after he hath killed hath power to cast into hell; yea, I say unto you, fear him" (Luke 12:4-5).

Paul warned the Romans, "The wrath of God is revealed from heaven against all ungodliness and unrighteousness of men who hold (suppress) the truth in unrighteousness"

(1:18). All men intuitively know certain truths concerning God and his laws. Since these truths are self-evident, they must make a vigorous mental effort to resist them.

Chares Finney explained, "The human mind is so constituted that truth is its natural stimulus. This stimulus of truth would, if not restrained and held back, lead the mind to naturally obey God. A person holds back the truth through his own unrighteousness, when, for selfish reasons, he overrules and restrains truth's natural influence, and will not allow it to take possession and hold sway over his mind."

Men then, are condemned for having rejected the light of nature. But how much more guilty do they become when, having heard the gospel, they reject it as well, and restrain all efforts of the Holy Spirit to impress it on their minds. Finally men actually come to hate the truth and love the lies by which they live. Paul entreats, "despisest thou the riches of his goodness and forbearance and long-suffering; not knowing that the goodness of God leadeth thee to repentance? But after thy hardness and impenitent heart treasurest up unto thyself wrath against the day of wrath and revelation of the righteous judgment of God" (Rom.2:4-5).

Governor Felix sent for Paul and listened to him concerning faith in Christ, and as Paul "reasoned of righteousness, temperance and of judgment to come, Felix trembled" (Acts 24:24-25). Because Paul addressed the issues which drew the convicting power of the Holy Spirit, Felix became alarmed and terrified. But he suppressed truth's natural influence and would not allow it to rule his life. He took advantage of God's forbearance and longsuffering and sent Paul away saying, "When I have a convenient season, I will call for thee."

There are limits even to God's patience. He suffers much, but the longer the gavel of his judgment is held back, the harder it will fall. Prideful Felix loved the riches of his position, more than the riches of God's goodness. "Another time," he said. But Felix may well have had his day of visitation.

God Hates Sinners

Just about any modern preacher having an opportunity to speak to a man of such prominence as Felix would emphasize Jesus' love. Actually, love is the predominant theme of modern evangelical preaching. But it is astounding to note that the word love is not once mentioned in the Book of Acts. The apostles, no doubt, were always motivated by love, and so must we be. But this does not mean that we should always speak of love.

We often hear that God loves the sinner, but hates the sin. But the Scriptures teach that God has a holy hatred for all workers of iniquity (Psalm 5:5). When an unawakened sinner is told that God loves him, he usually assumes that, to some extent, God is pleased with him and willing to relate to him just as he is. It has been said, "That God loves the fornicator, but hates the fornication. He loves the drunkard, but hates the drunkenness." This is absurd. Actions have no moral character apart from the actor. God does not hate and disapprove merely of the sin, but of the sinner himself.

Charles Finney explains, "The very thing that God hates and disapproves is not the mere event--the thing done in distinction from the doer; but it is the doer himself. It grieves and displeases God that a rational moral agent under his government should array himself against his own God and Father, against all that is right and just in the universe. This is the thing that offends God. The sinner himself is the direct and only object of his anger."

The Psalmist warned, "If he (the wicked) turn not, he (God) will whet his sword; he hath bent his bow, and made it ready" (Psalm 7:12) God does not shoot the sin, but the sinner. If God loves the sinner, but merely hates the sin, why, on Judgment Day, does he not just throw all sin into hell and take all sinners to heaven? It is ridiculous to believe that sin exists independently of the sinner.

God's hatred is not rooted in malice, but in benevolence. He does love the sinner in the sense the he wills his good (John 3:16). But he only has an abiding love (a relationship) with those who love and obey him (John 14:21; Prov. 8:17). The world and most of the church have little appreciation for God's holy character. They demean God by giving the impression that he loves all men the same way.

Alexander Maclaren cautions, "Let us take care, lest for the sake of seeming to preserve the impartiality of God's love, we have destroyed all in him that makes his love worth having. If to him the good and the bad, the men who fear him and the men who fear him not, are equally satisfactory, and, in the same manner, the objects of an equal love, then he is not a God that has pleasure in righteousness; and if he is not a God for us to trust."

The Holy Spirit does not woo the sinner as a man would a maiden. He does not appeal to the sinner's feelings, but to his mind (Isaiah 1:18). The Holy Spirit is viewed in Scripture as convicting, striving, reproving and even battling with the sinner. The Holy Spirit represents an offended Father to a rebellious son. The spirit reasons with the sinner to return home, but strictly on the Father's terms.

Yes, Revelation 3:20 pictures the Lord standing at the door of the sinner's heart knocking, but the wider picture must be seen. In the preceding verse the Spirit demonstrates, "As many as I love, I rebuke and chasten: be zealous therefore, and repent." We hear none of this nonsense that he will accept the sinner just as he is. Telling a hardened sinner that God loves him usually quenches the convicting influence of the Holy Spirit. Sinners first need to know that "God is angry with the wicked every day" (Psalm 7:11).

"The fear of the Lord is the beginning of knowledge" (Proverbs 1:7). Of course, the end of knowledge is love. But too often today we are trying to start the sinner at the finishing line (love), rather than at the starting line (fear). There are six references to the fear of God in the Book of Acts.

The Conscience

Paul reminded the Corinthians that we must all appear before the Judgment Seat of Christ; that everyone may receive the things done in his body, according to that which he has done: whether it be good or bad. "Knowing therefore the terror of the Lord, we persuade men; but we are made manifest unto God; and I trust also are made manifest in your consciences" (II Corinthians 5:11). By revealing himself to men's consciences, Paul prepared the way for the Holy Spirit to convict them of sin, righteousness and judgment. The conscience is man's moral sense. It is the faculty of the soul which pronounces on the character of our actions. *Conscience* is defined as "the faculty, power or principle within us, which decides on the lawfulness or the unlawfulness of our own actions and affections, and instantly condemns or approves them."

God has raised a Judgment Seat in every man's soul, which in some way answers to and prepares for the sentence the Holy Spirit pronounces on man's action. Whether it be good or bad. Every sinner stands condemned before his own Judgment Seat. Conscience judges him according to his works, independently of all creeds and theories. The modern gospel attempts to set aside this sentence, telling man that he should not judge himself by his actions, but according to his beliefs. But the conscience asserts itself and remorselessly holds up man's sin and points to coming retribution.

Conscience is an independent witness standing between God and man. This witness cannot be tampered with or bribed. This is the one human faculty that cannot be subdued. The conscience stands alone, taking sides against a man whenever he denies its sentence. It bears witness against him when he offends its integrity. As much as a person may attempt to deny the verdict of conscience and suppress its voice, still it smolders in the deep recesses of the soul; it whispers, "Guilty, guilty, guilty!"

Times when the sinner thinks he has succeeded in escaping the testimony of conscience, the Holy Spirit fans its embers--perhaps through a conversation, a sermon, a tract or a providential event and the conscience bellows, "GUILTY, GUILTY, GUILTY!"

The voice of conscience tormented King Saul and Judas that they were driven to suicide. How vital for man to confess and receive the Lord's pardon, as did Saul of Tarsus! After receiving the forgiveness of sins, he who had persecuted the church was able to testify before Felix that he had "a conscience void of offence toward God, and men" (Acts 24:16). There is no greater satisfaction than to have the peace of mind found in a clear conscience.

Probation

Prior to the 20th Century's modernism, Saint Paul and many Christian writers believed that man presently is in a state of probation. *Probation* is defined as "moral trial; the state of man in the present life, in which he has the opportunity of proving his character and being qualified for a happier state." Writers of old understood that probation only ended with the article of death.

The 18th-century theologian, Joseph Bellamy, said,

We are designed by God our Maker for an endless existence. In this present life we just enter upon being, and are in a state introductory to a never-ending duration in another world, where we are to be forever unspeakably happy or miserable, according to our present conduct. This is designed for a state of probation, and that for a state of rewards and punishments. We are now on trial, and God's eye is upon every movement; and the picture of ourselves which we exhibit in our conduct, the whole of it take together, will give our proper character and determine our state forever.

Judgment at the House of God

Peter understood the ministry of the Holy Spirit to convince believers of judgment: "for the time is come that judgment must begin at the house of God: and if it first begin at us, what shall the end be of them that obey not the gospel of God?" (I Peter 4:17). The manifestation of the gift of discerning of spirits operated through Peter when he exposed Ananias and Sapphira for lying to the Holy Ghost. As a result, "great fear came upon all the church" (Acts 5:11).

One of the greatest needs of our generation is to have mature men, "whose senses and mental faculties are trained by practice to discriminate and distinguish between what is morally good and noble, and what is evil and contrary, either to divine or human law" (Hebrews 5:14, Amplified).

Highly visible ministries regularly hosted men who were advertised as the most mighty and gifted men of God of our generation, but ironically, the sin was not exposed by them, but by the world or jealous competitors. Afterwards, the prophets of God unscrupulously scurried about to limit the damage and excuse the sin.

The Spirit of the Lord will expose sin one way or another. The Psalmist declared, "The Lord is known by the judgment he executeth" (Psalm 9:16). When hypocrisy is exposed, the people should be encouraged. God's judgment will always further the cause of Christ and strengthen the true church. Men's kingdoms may be ruined by God's judgments, but God's kingdom will always be glorified.

Jeremiah challenged the people "to run to and fro through the streets to find a man that executeth judgment." But none could be found. Even the great men had rejected the judgment of the Lord. The prophets and the priests refused to judge righteously; they passed over the deeds of the wicked; they had grown rich and become great by soothing the people. Jeremiah lamented, "My people love to have it so" (Jer. 5:31).

And so it is today. Professing Christians are satisfied with the lowly state of the church because they are allowed to continue in their sins, without reproof or restraint. People are so infatuated with personality-charged leaders that they willingly abandon themselves to blind guides and refuse to listen to those who still try to hold up a righteous standard and point to the old paths. "Yea, the stork in the heaven knoweth her appointed times; and the turtle and the crane and the swallow observe the time of their coming; but my people know not the judgment of the Lord" (Jer.8:7).

In the charismatic church at Corinth there was a notorious case of a fornicator, who was having an illicit relationship with his father's wife. The church had done nothing about it. If the church's attitude then was anything like its modern counterpart, the brethren were probably saying, "Let's just love the brother, and let the Holy Spirit take care of his sin." There was likely another group anxiously wanting to take authority, and "cast the demon of lust out of the brother in Jesus' name."

However, Paul's solution was not to cast out the devil, but "to deliver such a one unto Satan for the destruction of the flesh, that the spirit may be saved in the day of the Lord Jesus" (I Corinthians 5:5).

Paul judged the man; and he expected the church to cease treating him as a brother, to excommunicate him and anyone else who professed to be Christian but was a fornicator, covetous, and idolatrous, a railer, a drunkard, or an extortionist. They were not to even eat with such hypocrites.

If the church would start judging those that are within, it would promote a revival, but not before a great purging. How can the world be convinced that God is a God of judgment, when it is obvious that even the church does not believe in judging?

Paul had enough problems getting the church to accept his ministry and apostolic authority while he lived a blameless life. Suppose he had been exposed as a fornicator or extortioner. Even after a tearful confession, would he ever have been accepted again as a leader and minister? No. It could have provided the church with just the excuse it needed to get rid of this troublesome fellow who seemed to be always condemning. Yet today, ministers can fornicate, change wives, engage in highly questionable financial dealings and still be accepted as superstars in the body of Christ.

It's time that Christians judge themselves, in the light of the truth and according to the standard of "holiness, without which no man shall see the Lord" (Hebrews12:14). Those who are not obeying the gospel but are continuing to sin, need either to repent and start living righteously--thus qualifying for the name *Christian*--or cease playing the hypocrite by naming the name of Christ.

"Examine yourselves, whether ye be in the faith: prove your own selves. Know ye not your own selves, how that Jesus Christ is in you, except ye be reprobates?" (II Corinthians13:5).

And hereby we do know that we know him, if we keep his commandments. He that saith, 'I know him,' and keepeth not his commandments, is a liar, and the truth is not in him. But whoso keepeth his word, in him verily is the love of God perfected: hereby know we that we are in him (I John 2:3-5).

He can only be in us if we are in him. And the proof that we are in him is our obedience to him.

Christians Ought to Judge

Once we have judged ourselves, and are walking in the light we have, we need to start judging the world. "Do ye not know that the saints [Christians] shall judge the world? Know ye not that we shall judge angels? How much more things that pertain to this life?" (I Corinthians 6:2-3).

Alas, few know this! The world has quoted to the church, "Judge not, that ye not be judged" (Matthew 7:1). The church has accepted this admonition and has been deceived into thinking it should judge no one. But in this passage Jesus was merely rebuking hypocrites for their unfair judgments. "Thou hypocrite, first cast out the beam out of thine own eye, and then shalt thou see clearly to cast out the mote out of thy brother's eye" (Matthew 7:5).

The Christian, through repentance and faith in Christ, has cast the beam out of his own eye. Now he can see clearly to cast the mote (sin) out of others because his judgment is no longer blurred by his own sin. Jesus warned against false prophets. How can one recognize a false messenger if one does not judge?

A hypocrite is one who condemns others for what he himself does. Paul firmly reproved religious pretenders in Romans 2: "Therefore thou art inexcusable, O man, whosoever thou art that judgest: for wherein thou judgest another, thou condemnest thyself; for thou that judgest doest the same things." What are these same things? Paul listed, at the end of Chapter 1, the sinful things that bring the judgment of God:

"Being filled with all unrighteousness, fornication, wickedness, covetousness, maliciousness; full of envy, murder, debate, deceit, malignity; whisperers, backbiters, haters of God, despiteful, proud, boasters, inventors of evil things, disobedient to parents, without understanding, covenant breakers, without natural affection, implacable, unmerciful: who knowing the judgment of God, that they which commit such things are worthy of death, not only do the same, but have pleasure in them that do them (Romans 1:29-32).

Anyone doing these things, has no right to call himself a Christian, or to judge others who do them.

So few in our generation appreciate the goodness of the Holy Spirit in leading the sinner to repentance—through unctioning preachers to reprove sin, calling men to holy living, and warning of God's judgment. The Psalmist understood this anointing of the saints: "Let the righteous smite me; it shall be a kindness: and let him reprove me; it shall be an excellent oil, which shall not break my head: for yet my prayer also shall be in their calamities" (Psalm 141:5). Many evangelicals spare the truth today--all in the name of love, of course. They need to know the proverb, "Open rebuke is better than secret love" (Proverbs 27:5). Paul admonishes us, we are to "have no fellowship with the unfruitful works of darkness, but rather reprove them" (Ephesian 5:11).

Conviction is the oil that lights the eternal flame of the Holy Spirit within the human soul. It is excellent oil, but it is rarely valued. In fact, most clergymen seem to think it is their calling to carry around buckets of water to dilute the oil, lest a flame be kindled.

Dousing Conviction's Flame

Mark, a college freshman, had spent hours listening to us preach open-air on the campus lawn at The Ohio State University. He began to confide in my wife, Cindy, about his conviction of sin. One Friday after several days of discussions, he began to talk as if he were ripe for salvation. His conversation gave all indication that he was convinced of sin, righteousness and judgment. He admitted that a total surrender of his will to Jesus Christ was his only hope. Cindy did not pray the sinner's prayer with Mark, but made it clear that salvation was his choice, and he could and should repent immediately. She talked with excitement about Mark that weekend, feeling sure he would become a Christian.

But, Monday, a meeting with Mark brought bitter disappointment. Mark was a Catholic, and he had made the mistake of seeking the counsel of his priest over the weekend. Mr. Priest greeted Mark with a friendly smile and a warm handshake and ushered him into his air-conditioned office where buckets of water were waiting to douse the convicting sparks of the Holy Spirit.

Mark admitted to us that he had been an inch away from salvation, but the priest had talked him out of it.

This is not an isolated episode. I have seen this happen many times over the years. Students will hear us preach and become seriously troubled over the condition of their souls. They naturally seek advice from the minister, priest or rabbi of the religion of their parents. The clergyman scoffs at the preaching of judgment, calls us extremists and assures the troubled soul that God loves and forgives all. "You have nothing to fear," he says, as they race toward a fiery judgment.

The Terror of the Lord

Of course, it must be noted that opposition to preaching God's judgment against sinners is nothing new. Nathaniel W. Taylor, professor of theology at Yale College, observed early in the 19th century,

Of all kinds of preaching, there is perhaps none so unpopular-none the propriety of which is so frequently denied, none the salutary influence of which is so imperfectly understood-as what is commonly termed the preaching of terror. The fact that the Word if God abounds in the demonstrations of his wrath against sin, decides, beyond a moment's debate, that some highly important end is the design of these awful threatenings.

Paul and Barnabas appreciated the necessity of judging the wicked. When they were preaching on the Isle of Paphos, the deputy of the country called for them because he wanted to learn the Word of God. But a certain sorcerer, a false prophet, a Jew named Barjesus, stood against the apostles, trying to turn away the deputy from the faith. Then Paul, filled with the Holy Ghost, looked him straight in the eyes, and said:

O full of all subtility and all mischief, thou child of the devil, thou enemy of all righteousness, wilt thou not cease to pervert the right ways of the Lord? And now, behold, the hand of the Lord is upon thee, and thou shalt be blind, not seeing the sun for a season (Acts 13:9-11).

Immediately, Barjesus lost his sight, and he had to find someone to lead him by the hand. When the deputy saw what happened, he was convinced of the truth and believed, "...being astonished at the doctrine of the Lord."

Adam Clark's commentary is incisive:

The deputy is struck with astonishment as Barjesus was struck with blindness. Thus the Word of God is a two-edged sword: it smites the sinner with judgment or compunction; and the sinner inquires after truth, with conviction of its own worth and excellence.

No doubt in your typical "Spirit-filled" church, most today would be astonished at such an incident because they have been falsely taught that God never afflicts, but that sickness, disease and affliction always come from the devil. But the inspired writer of Acts 13 makes clear that "the hand of the Lord" was upon the sorcerer. Like the deputy, serious seekers after the truth will appreciate the work of the Holy Spirit in convincing the world of judgment.

Sorcerer

Ministering on university campuses, I have encountered a number of sorcerers. Clint, a sophomore at Ohio State, turned out to be a cross between Simon the sorcerer and Bar-jesus. At our first meeting, Clint impressed me as being much more interested in and in tune with the spiritual world than the average college student. He was also quite a talker, full of personality, and I immediately liked him.

In the fall of 1987, Clint started coming to our home regularly for dinner and joining in our Bible studies. He took notes, asked good questions, made intelligent remarks and seemed to be a very teachable seeker. Within a month he claimed to have intellectually accepted the teachings of Christianity. At the same time it became obvious that Clint was involved in drugs and witchcraft, but I was not sure to what extent. Nevertheless, Cindy and I began to pray earnestly for Clint, and we had high hopes for his salvation.

In the meantime, a freshman girl named Terri had become interested in our ministry and started coming to the Bible studies. Terri was an attractive girl from a wealthy family. Upon first meeting, she gave the impression of an ideal college girl who "had it all together." It did not take many conversations to see, that in reality, she was frustrated, confused and empty. Soon Terri also began to give mental assent to the claims of Christianity. We could see the Holy Spirit working in Terri's life, and we prayed for her daily.

Clint and Terri had much in common, and they began to spend time together. Knowing this was not the wisest situation, I continued in hope and prayer for their souls.

Finally, the night before Halloween, Terri cried out to God for salvation. The next day she came to our home testifying of her new life in Christ. We all rejoiced with exceeding joy.

Within a couple of days, Clint also claimed conversion, He confessed to being heavily into witchcraft and the many forms of debauchery associated with it. I had some doubts about Clint's motives, but I determined to "believe all things."

We counseled Clint and Terri to read the Bible, come to church, seek the Lord in prayer and keep their relationship pure.

This advice was futile, as it became obvious that Clint's intentions were to seduce Terri away from the faith to do his bidding. An insecure girl like Terri was no match for a charmer like Clint, and she soon succumbed to an immoral relationship.

Like Barjesus, Clint turned out to be a child of the devil full of all subtlety and mischief and determined to pervert the ways of the Lord. To our bitter disappointment, Clint succeeded in turning Terri away from the faith.

Finally, Clint admitted that he had never been sorry for his sins against God. He had seen that Christianity was true and was the wisest way to live. Like Simon, Clint realized that the real power lies in Christianity. For a short season he "believed," but soon the quest for power overtook him. The Bible does not tell us what happened to Simon. As for Clint, we never saw him after January, 1988. Two years later we heard that Clint was apprehended and taken to a mental hospital in the state where his parents reside.

"But we are sure that the judgment of God is according to truth against them that commit such things" (Romans 2:2).

Prophets of Old

We live in perilous times in the midst of an adulterous and perverse generation. Men that are truly filled with the Holy Spirit need to seek the anointing that was in Jesus, who "loved righteousness, and hated iniquity" (Hebrews 1:9). The apostles and prophets were stirred in their spirits when they confronted sin and idolatry.

Isaiah cried,

The shew of their countenance doth witness against them; and they declare their sin as Sodom, they hide it not. Woe unto their soul! For they have rewarded evil unto themselves. Say ye to the righteous, that it shall be well with him: for they shall eat the fruit of their doings. Woe unto the wicked! It shall be ill with him: for the reward of his hands shall be given him (Isa.3:9-11).

Woe unto them that call evil good, and good evil; that put darkness for light, and light for darkness; that put bitter for sweet, and sweet for bitter! Woe unto them that are wise in their own eyes, and prudent in their own sight! Woe unto them that are mighty to drink wine, and men of strength to mingle strong drink: which justify the wicked for reward, and take away the righteousness of the righteous from him! Therefore as the fire devoureth the stubble, and the flame consumeth the chaff, so their root shall be as rottenness, and their blossom shall go up as dust; because they have cast away the law of the Lord of hosts, and despised the word of the Holy One of Israel (Isaiah 5:20-24).

"By *faith* Noah, being warned of God of things not seen as yet, moved with fear, prepared an ark to the saving of his house; by the which he *condemned* the world, and became heir of the righteousness which is by faith" (Hebrews11:7).

The Lord anointed Noah, a preacher of righteousness, to warn his wicked generation of God's impending judgment. God had already clearly stated, "My Spirit shall not always strive with man" (Genesis 6:3). The Holy Spirit and Noah worked together contending, struggling and battling for 120 years with that perverse generation. God called Noah and his family into the ark and shut the door. It is a dangerous thing to resist the Holy Spirit. If God would give up on the whole population of the world in Noah's day, how much more would he give up on people of this generation who are more guilty than they, because we have rejected more light than was ever shown them.

The prophets of old, with all their woes (and what is a woe, but a curse or a warning of misery and calamity to come?) must have heard that, "It is better to light a candle than to curse the darkness." The fact is, we must do both, as the Holy Spirit reveals throughout the Bible.

Professor N. W. Taylor explains the importance of God's judgment in converting a sinner:

If to lay before him the horrors of impending death, and the woes of a ruined eternity, will not lead him to ponder the paths of his feet- nothing can. Although the mere fear of suffering is not enough to excite holy affections, it is enough to bring him to a state where purer and higher motives may reach him. It is enough to force him to sober meditation and thoughtfulness--a point to which he would never have come without the con-straining influence of a threatened damnation.

It needs to be remembered that Jesus,

[Upbraided] the cities wherein most of his mighty works were done, because they repented not: 'Woe unto thee, Chorazin! Woe unto thee, Bethsaida! For if the mighty works, which were done in you, had been done in Tyre and Sidon, they would have repented long ago in sackcloth and ashes. But I say unto you, it shall be more tolerable for Tyre and Sidon at the Day of Judgment, than for you. And thou, Capernaum, which art exalted unto heaven, shalt be brought down to hell: for if the mighty works, which have been done in thee, had been done in Sodom, it would have remained until this day' (Matt. 11:20-23).

The churches and air waves are filled with popular preachers, many with elaborate eschatological charts, who seem to have everything figured out; but they miss the central purpose and message of prophecy, which is to bring men into a right relationship with God. Peter had a simple and clear prophetic message.

*But the day of the Lord will come as a thief
in the night; in the which the heavens shall
pass away with a great noise, and the ele-
ments shall melt with fervent heat, the earth
also and the works that are therein shall be
burned up. Seeing then that all these things
shall be dissolved, what manner of persons
ought ye to be in all holy conversation and
godliness (II Peter 3:10-11).*

In the Book of Revelation, John, popularly
known as the apostle of love, preached perhaps more judgment than any of the
prophets before him.

*And I saw another angel fly in the midst of
heaven, having the everlasting gospel to
preach unto them that dwell on the earth,
and to every nation, and kindred, and
tongue, and people, saying with a loud
voice, 'Fear God, and give glory to him; for
the hour of his judgment is come: and worship him that made heaven, and earth, and
the sea, and the fountains of waters'
(Rev.14:6-7).*

CONCLUSION: GOD'S PERPETUAL GRIEF

When the Lord fulfilled his promise on the Day of the Pentecost by sending the Comforter to indwell the believers, he must have had great prospects for the church subduing the world into his righteous kingdom. The church started so brilliantly that, despite fierce opposition and the martyrdom of her leaders, within a generation she had established bases throughout the known world.

The Book of Acts records the magnificent militancy and glorious victories of the church fighting on the side of the Holy Spirit against an unbelieving world, by convicting of sin, righteousness and judgment as Jesus promised. The Comforter was omnipresent to empower and console the Christians in their battles and persecutions and to guide them into all truth. But no sooner than these churches were established, false doctrine, sin and worldliness crept in, and seriously weakened and, in some cases, virtually took over the churches that had become divisive, lukewarm and plagued with the same sins that were in the world. How greatly disappointed the Holy Spirit must have been to have to contend with those whom he had expected to comfort.

The problems with the churches that the apostles addressed have remained more or less in the visible body of Christ unto our day. There have been periods of revival, then decline; but by and large, in view of the Great Commission to make disciples of the nations, the church must be a frustration to the Holy Spirit.

Thankfully, there has always been an obedient remnant in whom the Holy Spirit has been able to delight. This remnant is the true church.

In Isaiah, Chapter 5, we have a beautiful parable expressing the tender care of God for his people, and their unworthy returns for his goodness:

Now will I sing to my well-beloved a song of my beloved touching his vineyard. My well-beloved hath a vineyard in a very fruitful hill. And he fenced it, and gathered out the stones thereof, and planted it with the choic-

est vine, and built a tower in the midst of it, and also made a wine press therein: and he looked that it should bring forth grapes, and it brought forth wild grapes. And now, O inhabitants of Jerusalem, and men of Judah, judge, I pray you, betwixt me and my vineyard. What could have been done more to my vineyard, that I have not done in it? Wherefore, when I looked that it should bring forth grapes, brought it forth wild grapes? (Isaiah 5:1-4).

What a sad song! Our great God had planted and nurtured Israel for generations and had expected and intended them to be a great people who would reflect his character by doing justly and living righteously, but they had turned out to be a rebellious and idolatrous people. God's consuming desire was to rejoice over his people in love, but this was not possible in their rebellion. God wondered what more he could do for his vineyard than he had already done.

Centuries later God sent his Son, his well-beloved, unto them, saying, "They will reverence my son." But they killed the Son and threw him out of the vineyard. "What shall therefore the lord of the vineyard do? He will come and destroy the husbandmen, and will give the vineyard unto others" (Mark 12:6-9).

For two millenniums the church has been the vineyard, but alas, it has provided as much grief to God as Israel. God looks for righteousness and judgment in the church, but finds only a remnant interested in these issues. One wonders, where is the God of judgment today? But it needs to be understood that it is not God's inclination to be judgmental and pour out his wrath upon man. He longs to express his loving nature revealing his mercy and forgiveness to man.

The late Gordon Olson, a Charles Finney scholar and theologian, explained the relationship between God's judgment and his love:

The Bible reveals that 'God is love' (I John 4:8), by which we understand that God is benevolently attached to virtue and goodness. This is not a state of sentimentality, but a devotion to truth and righteousness. Wrath is a product of love provoked to indignation by wrong moral action of others. But wrath is a necessary intrusion into Divine Personalities, whereas love and complacency is their essential character. Love is spontaneous and free flowing. Wrath is provoked and climatic as occasions demand. Wrath therefore must be an unhappy activity in the experience of the God-head.

Hosea expresses God's puzzlement in how to act toward his backsliding people, "How shall I deliver thee, Israel? How shall I make thee as Admah? How shall I set thee as Zeboim? Mine heart is turned within me, my repentings are kindled together" (Hosea 11:8). Like a loving but bewildered parent, God is tossed between pouring out the judgment which the people deserve and the mercy which he longs to extend. Justice demands punishment, but mercy pleads for life. God's heart is oppressed by the shallow repentance. He is weary from having so frequently to change his purpose. How shall he resolve this conflict in his mind?

He decides, "I will not execute the fierceness of mine anger, I will not return to destroy Ephraim: for I am God, and not man; the Holy One in the midst of thee: and I will not enter into the city" (Hosea 11:9). Mercy triumphs over judgment. Ephraim is spared, at least for a time, for God is not affected by human caprices.

How touching and revealing are these two verses from Hosea. Judgment is God's strange work. The forbearance and longsuffering of God is taken for granted, abused and rarely understood even by his prophets. In recent history, we have had sincere men of God, preachers of righteousness, prophesy impending judgment on the church and America, which did not come to pass. They made the serious mistake of assuming God's ways were man's ways.

On the contrary, it is a deadly mistake to suppose that God cannot be provoked to wrath. Because God is a being who loves righteousness, he must eventually judge sinners in order to demonstrate his holy hatred of sin and to uphold his moral government.

Man's sin has brought about all human suffering in the world and endless grief to God. The Psalmist summarizes Israel's rebellious history by lamenting, "How oft did they provoke him in the wilderness, and grieve him in the desert!" (Psalm 78:40).

Consequently, God had to bring terrible judgments upon his people. Even in the Promised Land, the Israelite people continued to bring great pain to God by their disobedience. Isaiah cries, "But they rebelled, and vexed his Holy Spirit: therefore he was turned to be their enemy, and he fought against them" (Isaiah 63:10).

The Apostle Paul was very sensitive to the sensibilities of the Holy Spirit. It is likely he had in mind the words of David and Isaiah when he warned the church at Ephesus, "Grieve not the Holy Spirit of God, whereby ye are sealed unto the day of redemption" (Ephesians 4:30), by giving way to any wrong temper, unholy word or unrighteous action.

Multitudes in the church are deceived into thinking that sin will not condemn those who have been born again because they are sealed by the Holy Spirit. But they need to remember that they were sealed after hearing and believing the truth. Should they reject the truth and return to sin, the seal or bond between the believer and God is broken. Alas, those that are showing contempt to the Spirit of Grace will not see the day of redemption, but only the day of perdition.

But "…mercy rejoiceth against judgment" (James 2:13). God "is longsuffering to us, not willing that any should perish, but that all should come to repentance" (II Peter 3:9).

The Advocate's Plea

O reader, is there any sin in your life? Then turn from it unto Jesus Christ, who suffered the consequences of man's sin on the cross of Calvary. "For he hath made him to be sin for us, who knew no sin; that we might be made the righteousness of God in him" (II Corinthians 5:21).

"That if thou shalt confess with thy mouth the Lord Jesus, and shalt believe in thine heart that God hath raised him from the dead, thou shalt be saved" (Romans10:9).

So often we hear testimonies that go something like this: "Three years ago Jesus became my Savior; three months ago he became Lord of my life." Not so! Jesus does not become Savior until he becomes Lord.

"And why call ye me, 'Lord, Lord', and do not things which I say?" (Luke 6:46).

Jesus utterly denounced sinning religion: "Ye hypocrites, well did Esaias prophesy of you, saying, 'this people draweth nigh unto me with their mouth, and honoureth me with their lips; but their heart is far from me'" (Matthew 15:7-8).

True religion comes from the heart (purpose of the will). "For with the heart man believeth unto righteousness" (Romans10:10).

What does it mean to believe from the heart? To have your will submitted to God's will. What one believes, in the Biblical sense, are those convictions, morals and principles by which he lives, as opposed to those he merely entertains or prefers. The evidence that a man believes from his heart is a righteous, obedient life. Nothing short of this should be considered salvation.

Dear Reader, don't quench the work of the Holy Spirit in your life, but call upon Jesus' name for salvation today!

Other Titles by Bro. Jed Smock

Who Will Rise Up? *A biographical classic on open-air evangelism*

Walking in the Spirit *A Liberating Commentary of Romans 6, 7&8*

Christ Triumphant, *The Battle of the Ages*

The Mystery of Christ Revealed: *The Key to Understanding Predestination*

Website: brojed.org

Email: brojed@aol.com

cindysmock@aol.com

Facebook: Jed Smock (Bro. Jed)

YouTube: Brother Jed Channel

Phone 573-999-0347   573-999-0346

Address:

Brother Jed Smock

The Campus Ministry USA

PO Box 3845

Terre Haute IN 47803

If you would like to help CMUSA continue to reach college students with this Gospel of Jesus Christ, you may send a gift to the above address or give through PayPal on our website. Thank you and pray for us. **Bro Jed**